LEVEL **1**

W0099570

The Boy from Yesterday

John Davage

Richmond READERS

R Richmond READERS

LEVEL 1

(500 headwords)

Maria's Dilemma
Oscar
Jack's Game
The Boy from Yesterday
The Black Mountain

LEVEL 2

(800 headwords)

Jason Causes Chaos
Craigen Castle Mystery
The Road through the Hills and othes stories
Where's Mauriac?
Saturday Storm

LEVEL 3

(1200 headwords)

A Trip to the Stars
Dr Jekyll and Mr Hyde
The Canterville Ghost and Other Stories
Cold Feet
Frankenstein

LEVEL 4

(1800 headwords)

A Trip to London
Dracula
Jane Eyre
The Adventures of Tom Sawyer
Sense and Sensibility

LEVEL 5

(2600+ headwords)

Steve Jobs: the man behind Apple
Elizabeth II The Diamond Queen

The Boy from Yesterday

Sea Bird Cottage is the ideal place for a holiday. That's what Mrs Dale and her children think when they first arrive. But the cottage has a sad history. What are the noises they hear at night? Who is the mysterious figure in the garden? And who is the boy from yesterday?

....

John Davage writes both fiction and non-fiction and has adapted many books for students learning English as a foreign language. He lives near the sea, in Dorset, in the South of England.

LEVEL **1**

CHAPTER 1
Sea Bird Cottage

Pattie Dale and her brother Will looked out of the car window. There was the cottage*. It was small and dark under the trees.

'It says Sea Bird Cottage on the wall,' Will said.

'Then that's our cottage,' their mother said. She opened the car door and got out. 'Well, it's near the sea, and it's not too far from the centre of the village. That's good.'

Just then, a big woman with a red, smiling* face came out of the front door of the cottage. 'Hello,' she said. 'You're Mrs Dale, aren't you? I'm Mrs Burns. I work for Mr Webb, up at the big house. This is his cottage.' She watched Pattie and Will get out of the car. 'How long are you staying? A week?'

'Yes,' Mrs Dale said. 'It's only a short holiday.'

'We would like it to be longer,' Pattie said.

'Long holidays are expensive,' Mrs Dale said. She looked at Mrs Burns. 'My husband died two years ago, and I work...'

'You work too hard!' Will said, quickly. 'You need a good holiday.'

Just then, a big woman with a red, smiling face came out of the door of the cottage.

'And we're going to have a good holiday,' Mrs Dale said, and she smiled.

They looked at 'the big house' - Sea Bird House - through the trees behind the cottage. Mrs Burns said, 'Mr Webb lives in the house with his grandson*. Roger is fifteen. His mother and father are working in Canada at the moment.'

'We're fifteen, too,' said Pattie. Then she explained, 'We're twins*.'

They took their things out of the car and went into the cottage. The rooms were small and dark, but everything was clean. There was a table under one of the windows. Mrs Dale went across and put her small computer on it.

Mrs Burns looked at it. 'Are you going to do some work?' she asked, surprised.

Mrs Dale smiled. 'I'm a writer,' she said. 'This is really a working holiday for me. I must finish writing a book.'

'But you're going to have a holiday, too,' Pattie said. 'Will and I can go to the village for food, and make breakfast and dinner.'

'And we can make the beds, and...' Will began to say.

'Yes, yes!' Mrs Dale said, laughing. 'All right. Thank you, both of you.'

She went to the car again, and Mrs Burns followed* her. Pattie and Will ran up the stairs* to look at the two bedrooms.

'Mum and I are going to have the big room,' Pattie said.

Will went into his bedroom and walked across to the window. 'I can see the sea!' he shouted.

Pattie came to look. She saw the cliffs and the grey sea through the trees.

They looked down and saw Mrs Burns with their mother in the garden.

'What's Mrs Burns talking about?' Will said.

'I don't know,' Pattie said, 'but Mum looks very serious.'

They went down the stairs, and their mother came into the cottage.

She saw the cliffs and the grey sea through the trees.

'The bedrooms are nice,' Pattie said. 'Will can see the sea from his.'

'What?' Mrs Dale said.

'What's the matter?' Will said.

'Oh ... er ... nothing,' Mrs Dale said. 'It was something Mrs Burns said.'

'What?' Will asked.

'It's not important,' Mrs Dale said.

'A secret*?' Pattie asked.

'Yes,' Mrs Dale said. 'A secret.'

—— CHAPTER 2 ——
A Telephone Call

It rained for the next two days. Pattie and Will went out for walks on the beach and along the cliffs. But they got very wet* and cold, and soon came back to the cottage to read books and watch television.

'What does Roger do here on rainy days?' Will said. It was late in the afternoon, on the third day. 'It's not a very exciting village, and there's no cinema here.'

'Roger?' Pattie said.

'Mr Webb's grandson.' Will said.

'Oh, yes,' Pattie said. 'Did you see him yesterday, or the day before yesterday?'

'No,' Will said. 'Did you?'

'No,' Pattie said.

Mrs Dale sat next to the window and worked on her computer. Sometimes she looked out into the garden. She could see the gardens near the big house.

'There's a cinema in the next town,' she said. 'We can go this evening.'

A little later, the telephone rang. Mrs Dale answered it. Pattie and Will went into the kitchen. Will started to make dinner, and Pattie watched him.

'That's too much pasta,' Pattie said. 'We can't eat all that.'

'I can,' Will said. 'I'm hungry.'

'And we don't need so much meat,' Pattie said. 'There are three of us for dinner, not ten!'

'I'm making this dinner, not you!' Will said. 'And I...'

Mrs Dale ran into the kitchen. Her face was white. 'That was your grandfather* on the phone,' she said.

'Grandad?' Pattie said. 'What's wrong?'

'Your grandmother* is ill,' Mrs Dale said. 'She's in hospital. I must go back home tonight.'

'Shall we come?' Pattie asked.

'No,' her mother said. 'No, you can't help. And perhaps I can come back in one or two days. Can you get your food, and...?'

'Yes, of course,' Will said, 'Don't worry* about us, Mum.'

'Tell Mrs Burns...' his mother began to say.

'It's OK, Mum, we can tell her,' Pattie said. 'Don't worry.'

Mrs Dale went to her bedroom to put some clothes in a bag. She came down two minutes later. She looked at her watch*. 'I can be at the hospital in three hours,' she said.

'Will you telephone us from there?' Pattie asked.

'Yes, all right,' Mrs Dale said.

They watched her run across to the car in the rain, and drive away.

'I'm worried about Gran,' Will said. 'Do you think she's going to die?'

'No!' Pattie said quickly. Then she said more slowly, 'I don't know, Will. But there's nothing we can do.'

■ ■ ■

Late that night, their mother phoned from the hospital. 'Gran is the same,' she told Pattie. 'The doctor says that the next few days are important.'

'How is Grandad?' Pattie asked.

'He's OK,' Mrs Dale said. 'But he needs me at the moment, and I want to stay here.'

'Then you must stay with him,' Pattie said.

'Oh ... and I wanted to say ... the cottage...' Mrs Dale began to say, but stopped.

'Yes?' Pattie said.

'Oh ... nothing. It doesn't matter,' Mrs Dale said.

'Don't worry about us, Mum,' Pattie said. 'We're OK.'

But suddenly* Sea Bird Cottage was very quiet and empty.

■ ■ ■

At five o'clock the next morning, Will sat* up in bed.

'What's that noise*?' he thought*.

He got out of bed and went across to the bedroom window. It was raining hard, and there was a strong wind*. The branch of a tree hit his window.

It was raining hard, and there was a strong wind. The branch of a tree hit his window.

Will could not go to sleep after that. At half-past five, he went to the kitchen and made a cup of coffee. He went to the window and looked out. There were big pools of water all over the garden.

Then he heard another noise. 'Something is moving,' he thought. 'Something is under the cottage!' He looked down. 'Perhaps there's a cellar*. But where is the cellar door? Did I hear a noise? Perhaps it was the rain or the wind.'

But he knew that it wasn't.

─── CHAPTER 3 ───
The Boy in the Garden

At six o'clock, Pattie got out of bed and went across to her bedroom window.

'It's raining again!' she thought. She looked across the garden. 'We need to buy food from the village this morning. We're going to get wet!'

Then she saw someone. A figure moved between the trees.

Then she saw someone. A figure moved between the trees.

The boy wore* black trousers, a grey shirt, and some heavy shoes. But he had no coat. He moved slowly, very slowly, through the trees. Pattie could not see his face.

'Who is it?' Pattie thought. 'Of course, it's Roger! Mr Webb's grandson.'

She watched him for another minute or two.

Then, suddenly, he wasn't there!

■ ■ ■

'I think it was Roger,' Pattie said.

It was breakfast time.

'Did he see you?' Will asked.

'No, he didn't look at the cottage,' Pattie said. 'But there was something...'

'What?' Will said.

'His clothes,' Pattie said. 'They were ... strange*. They were clothes that people wore a long time ago.'

'Maybe Roger likes old clothes,' Will said.

He finished his breakfast and got up. Suddenly, he heard the noise again. The noise under the cottage.

'What's that?' Pattie said.

'I don't know,' Will said. 'I heard it earlier. I think it's something in the cellar.'

'What cellar?' Pattie said.

They looked for a cellar door for the next ten minutes.

But they did not find one.

Their mother phoned again, an hour later. 'Gran is a

little better,' Mrs Dale said to Pattie. 'But I'm going to stay here today. Are you all right?'

'We're OK, don't worry, Mum,' Pattie said.

'You need some food,' Mrs Dale began to say.

'We're going to the village shop later,' Pattie said.

'Is everything all right?' Mrs Dale asked.

'What do you mean?' Pattie said.

'At the cottage,' Mrs Dale said. 'Is everything all right at the cottage?'

Pattie thought about the strange noises, but she said, 'Yes, everything is all right. Give our love to Gran and Grandad.'

Twenty minutes later, she and Will went out. The rain was still very heavy and they walked through big pools of water to get across the garden. There was a stream next to the road, about twenty metres from the cottage. The water in the stream was very high.

'The water's nearly on the road,' Pattie said.

Will stopped and looked round.

'What's the matter?' Pattie asked.

'I saw somebody ... yes, look! In the trees!' he said.

Pattie looked. 'I don't see anybody,' she said.

'He's not there now,' Will said.

'He?' she said.

'A boy.' Will looked at Pattie, then said, 'Roger? Maybe he's watching us.'

'But ... why?' Pattie said.

'I don't know,' Will said.

———— CHAPTER **4** ————
The Picture

By the time they got to the village shop, they were both wet and cold.

'Let's get the things we need, then go back to the cottage,' Pattie said.

'OK,' Will said. 'I want to get out of these wet clothes.'

They got some vegetables, a big bottle of Coca Cola, and some other things. They were not in the shop for long. When they came out again, the road was like a river of rainwater and Pattie got water in her shoes.

They stopped in the doorway of another shop. There were a lot of old books, and old postcards and pictures of the village in the window. Pattie took off her shoes to get the water out of them.

Suddenly, Will said, 'Look, Pattie! Look at that picture!'

It was a small picture near the front of the window.

'It's a picture of Sea Bird House!' Pattie said.

There were some words under it: 'Sea Bird House, 1884. Some people call it "the smuggler's* house" because George Fenton, the smuggler, lived there.'

'Smugglers!' Will said. 'Do you think that smugglers lived in Sea Bird Cottage? Maybe they put the contraband* there.'

'Yes!' Pattie said. 'Maybe they put it in the cellar.'

'It's a picture of Sea Bird House!' Pattie said.

'But there isn't a cellar,' said Will. And then he remembered the strange noises. 'Or is there?'

The wind was much stronger now. It was difficult to walk. When they got nearer to the cottage, they saw that the stream was now much bigger. Water moved very fast from the stream into the road.

'My feet are going to be wet again!' Pattie shouted* into the wind.

'Look!' Will shouted back. 'Some of the road is breaking. All this water is making holes in the road. Can you see?'

The wind moved the trees over their heads. It was difficult to see the road in front of them because the rain was so heavy. Pattie carried the bag of vegetables

and other things. Will walked with his head down. He
didn't like the rain. He didn't want the rain in his face.
Water ran into the holes in the road.

Suddenly, Pattie heard Will shout, 'Aaaagh!'

And then he wasn't there!

'Will!' Pattie shouted. She began to run.

She saw a big hole in the road, and looked down.
Will was at the bottom of the hole!

Will was at the bottom of the hole!

'Will!' she shouted again. 'Are you all right?'

'My foot,' Will shouted. 'I can't stand on it.'

Pattie knelt on the ground. There was now a lot of
water in the hole. 'I must get him out before it's full of
water!' she thought.

'Give me your hand!' she shouted.

He put his hands up to her – but she was too far

away. She tried to get nearer, but she was afraid. She didn't want to fall into the hole too. Will put his arms up again.

'I can't...!' he began to say. Then more of the road fell* into the hole and over his head.

'Will! Will!' Pattie shouted.

'I ... I'm all right!' he shouted. 'But I must get out of here!'

'I need another person!' Pattie shouted. 'Will? Can you hear me? I'm going to get Mr Webb, or somebody.'

'All right!' Will shouted. She could see his face again now. 'But be quick!'

─────── CHAPTER **5** ───────

The Face

Pattie hit the door of Sea Bird House again and again.

'Please!' she shouted. 'Come to the door! Mr Webb! Mr Webb!'

After another minute, the door opened.

'What's the matter?' It was Mrs Burns.

'Is Mr Webb here?' Pattie said.

'Mr Webb went to London, yesterday,' said Mrs Burns. 'He is back tomorrow.'

'Please, you must help me,' Pattie said quickly. 'My brother fell into a hole, and I can't reach* him.'

Mrs Burns was surprised. 'A hole?'

'In the road near the cottage.' Pattie explained about the stream and the water and the broken road. 'You're tall. You can reach him,' she said. 'But we must be quick!'

■ ■ ■

Will was very cold now. There was more water in the hole. It was up round his knees now. His feet and trousers were wet. It was difficult to stand on his foot.

'Where's Pattie?' he thought.

Rain and stream-water came into the hole very fast. Suddenly, another part of the road fell into the hole, and Will put his hands over his head.

'Be quick, Pattie!' he thought. 'Be quick!'

How much time before...? He didn't want to think about it.

'Think about something different,' he said. 'What? Smugglers, yes! Think about smugglers.' He could see pictures inside his head...

...men are bringing brandy* from a boat and onto the beach. It is the middle of the night ... a black night ... it is windy ... the moon comes out from behind a cloud in the sky ... white faces look up ... they are afraid ... the boxes of brandy are heavy ... it is difficult for the men, and there are shouts ... heads move in the dark ... heads...

A head! Will looked up – and saw a head at the top of the hole. It was the boy! He had very black hair, and big, dark brown eyes.

'Help!' Will shouted. 'Roger! Help me!'

He could see pictures inside his head...

The boy did not speak. Slowly, he got down on the ground and put his arms into the hole.

Will reached up, and put his hands into the boy's hands. Then he saw the boy's face.

He could see through it! He could see the rain and the trees behind the boy's face!

■ ■ ■

Pattie and Mrs Burns ran through the pools of water in the cottage garden, then on into the road.

'Where...?' Mrs Burns began to say.

'Down there!' Pattie shouted. 'Under the trees. The hole is...' She stopped. She saw somebody in the road. 'Will?' she shouted. 'Will!' She ran towards him.

He looked up and saw them. 'Hello,' he said.

Will reached up and put his hands into the boy's hands.

Pattie looked at him. There was something strange about him. A strange, calm look on his face. 'How...?' she began to say.

'Can you help me? I can't get up,' he said. 'My foot...'

Pattie and Mrs Burns helped him.

'You're wet and cold,' Mrs Burns said. 'We must take you back to the cottage.'

They began to walk. Will didn't say anything, but two or three times he looked behind him.

'How did you get out of the hole?' Pattie asked.

Will looked at her, then looked away. 'The boy helped me,' he said. 'But his face...'

'Boy?' Mrs Burns said quickly. She looked at Will.

'What boy?'

'The boy in the garden,' he said to Pattie. 'Do you remember?'

'Roger?' Pattie said. 'Roger Webb?'

'No,' Mrs Burns said, quietly. 'No, not Roger. Roger is flying to Canada. He's going to see his parents for two weeks. Mr Webb took him to London yesterday, and they stayed at a hotel in London last night.' She looked at her watch. 'Roger's aeroplane left Heathrow Airport two hours ago.'

'Oh,' Will said.

'Then who was the boy?' Pattie said. 'I saw him in the cottage garden.'

'And I saw him earlier,' Will said. 'He had very black hair, and big, dark brown eyes.'

Mrs Burns was quiet for a moment or two. Then she said, 'It was Dan Fenton.'

'Fenton?' Will said. 'That's the name of the smuggler. We saw a picture in a shop in the village. George Fenton, the smuggler, lived at Sea Bird House, didn't he?'

'Yes. Dan Fenton was his son,' Mrs Burns said.

'Was his son?' Pattie said after a moment. 'You mean … the boy we saw … is dead?'

'Oh, yes,' Mrs Burns said. 'He died a hundred years ago. Everybody in the village knows the story.'

—— CHAPTER **6** ——
A Smuggler's Story

'A ghost*?' Will said.

'No,' Pattie said. 'No, it's not possible. You saw a ghost?'

'Yes,' Will said, slowly. 'Yes, it was a ghost. Because...'

'What?' Pattie said.

'I saw through him,' Will said. 'I saw the trees and the rain behind his face.'

Pattie's face went white. After a moment, she said, 'So Dan Fenton's ghost helped you?'

'Yes,' Will said. 'Yes, I think so.'

'Was Dan Fenton a smuggler, too?' Pattie asked Mrs Burns.

'No,' Mrs Burns said.

'Did he know that his father was a smuggler?' Will asked.

'He didn't know at first,' Mrs Burns said. 'But his father often went out late at night. He asked his father, "What do you do at night?" But his father got angry with all the questions, and Dan stopped asking them. Then, one night, he followed his father down to the beach. He secretly watched George Fenton and some other men carry brandy from a boat, and across the beach. And then Dan knew the truth. His father was a smuggler.'

'Was ... was it a windy night?' Will asked. He remembered the pictures inside his head.

'Yes,' Mrs Burns said. 'It was very windy. It was difficult for the men to get the brandy to the tunnel*.'

'Tunnel?' Pattie said.

'There was a tunnel under the cliff,' Mrs Burns said. 'It went under Sea Bird House, and on to the cellar of an inn* in the village.'

'Did Dan Fenton go into the tunnel?' Will asked.

'Yes,' Mrs Burns said. 'And he died in the tunnel.'

'How?' Pattie asked. 'How did he die in the tunnel?'

'He waited five minutes after the smugglers went into the tunnel,' Mrs Burns explained. 'Then he followed them. But the ground above the tunnel was very wet and heavy after weeks of rain. He walked for about three or four hundred metres, and then the ground fell in on top of him.'

'Oh!' Pattie said. She put her hands up to her face.

'The smugglers heard the ground fall into the tunnel. "We can't get through there again," one smuggler said. "Then we must make a new tunnel," George Fenton said. But he did not know that Dan was in the tunnel. Next morning, he found that Dan was not in his bed.'

'What did he do?' Will asked.

'He went to look for Dan on the beach, but he could not find him,' Mrs Burns said. 'Then he and some other men looked in every part of the village, and along every part of the cliffs and the beach. Of course, they didn't find Dan. At first, George didn't think about the tunnel. Then he remembered Dan's

Dan waited five minutes after the smugglers went into the tunnel. Then he followed them.

questions. And then he knew. Dan was in the tunnel.'

'Did they ever get Dan out?' Pattie asked.

'No,' Mrs Burns said. 'It was impossible. So they shut the tunnel up, and no one ever went there again.'

'Is the tunnel ... under the cottage?' Pattie asked. She thought about the strange noises.

'People say that it is,' Mrs Burns said.

'Is there a cellar under the cottage?' Will asked.

'Cellar?' Mrs Burns said. 'No, there's no cellar.'

'How old was Dan?' Pattie asked.

'Sixteen,' Mrs Burns said. 'People say they sometimes see his ghost near the cottage.'

'We did,' Pattie said, after a moment.

■ ■ ■

Mrs Dale came back the next morning. She got out of the car, and Pattie and Will went to meet her.

'Gran is much better,' she said to them. 'She is coming out of hospital on Friday.'

'That's great!' Pattie said.

'And now we can go on with our holiday,' Mrs Dale said. She smiled. 'Look, here's the sun!'

She was right. The weather was much better.

Will took his mother's bag out of the car.

'Is everything all right at the cottage?' Mrs Dale asked. 'I mean ... well...'

Pattie and Will smiled.

'It's OK, Mum,' Pattie said. 'We know the secret of Sea Bird Cottage now.'

'The secret that Mrs Burns told you the first day,' Will said.

'You ... you do?' Mrs Dale said.

'Yes, Mum,' Pattie said. 'We know that it has a ghost.'

'And we saw it,' said Will.

'What?' Mrs Dale said. 'Oh!'

'Yes,' Pattie said. 'It's a very nice ghost, isn't it, Will?'

'Oh, yes,' Will said. 'Very nice. It likes to help people.'

EXERCISES

A Comprehension

Chapter 1 Who in this chapter...

1 ...is a writer?
2 ...lives in Sea Bird House with his grandson?
3 ...tells Mrs Dale a secret?

Chapters 2 and 3 Who said or thought these words?

1 'It's not a very exciting village, and there's no cinema here.'
2 'The doctor says that the next few days are important.'
3 'That's too much pasta.'
4 'Perhaps there's a cellar. But where is the cellar door?'
5 'Of course, it's Roger!'
6 'Is everything all right at the cottage?'
7 'I saw somebody ... yes, look! In the trees!'

Chapters 4 and 5 Write answers to these questions.

1 What do Pattie and Will see in a shop window in the village?
2 Why do some people call Sea Bird House 'the smuggler's house'?
3 Why must Pattie get Will out of the hole quickly?
4 Who does Pattie get to help her?
5 Why is Roger flying to Canada?
6 Who is Dan Fenton?

Chapter 6 Are these sentences true (T) or false (F)?

1 Dan watched George Fenton and some other men carry brandy from a boat and across the beach.
2 The tunnel went under Sea Bird House.
3 Dan was fourteen years old.

B Working with Language

I Use these words to join the two halves of each sentence.

because   about   but   and

I Pattie got out of bed. Went across to her bedroom window.

2 There was a stream next to the road. Twenty metres from the cottage.

3 The rooms were small and dark. Everything was clean.

4 Some people call it 'the smuggler's house'. George Fenton, the smuggler, lived there.

2 Match the words below to the correct headings.

building   weather   family

grandmother   windy   twin   cottage   rain   inn
mother   shop   house   husband   cloud   sun

C Activities

I Do you believe in ghosts? Write 200 words to explain why you believe/don't believe in ghosts.

2 Are there any famous ghost stories from your country? Write about your favourite story.

3 Will and Pattie tell their mother about the boy from yesterday. What do they say to her? Write down their conversation.

GLOSSARY

brandy *(n)* a strong alcoholic drink

cellar *(n)* a room in the ground under a house

contraband *(n)* things that have been imported or exported illegally

cottage *(n)* a small house in the country

fell *(v)* past tense of *fall*

follow *(v)* walk behind someone, going in the same direction

ghost *(n)* a dead person that a living person can see

grandfather *(n)* the father of your father or mother; *informal* **grandad**

grandmother *(n)* the mother of your father or mother; *informal* **gran**

grandson *(n)* the son of your child

inn *(n)* a house or small hotel where you can buy drinks and meals

noise *(n)* something that you can hear, a loud sound

reach *(v)* move your arm forward so that you can touch something

sat *(v)* past tense of *sit*

secret *(n)* something that other people do not know

shout *(v)* speak strongly because you are afraid, or because you want to make someone far away hear you

smiling *(adj)* with a happy face

smuggler *(n)* someone who brings contraband into the country

stairs *(n)* a set of steps

strange *(adj)* something unusual that makes you feel surprised or afraid

suddenly *(adj)* if something happens suddenly, it happens very quickly

thought *(v)* past tense of *think*

tunnel *(n)* a long hole through the ground

twins *(n)* two children who have the same mother and are born at the same time

watch *(n)* something you wear on your arm which shows the time

wet *(adj)* with water or rain on it

wind *(n)* air that moves

wore *(v)* past tense of *wear*

worry *(v)* feel that something is wrong, or will be wrong